Dean and Tammie Carter

Outreach Christian Ministry

The Invisible Keys

Helping those who help others

Bad Choices, Good People

Bloomington, IN  Milton Keynes, UK

AuthorHouse™
1663 Liberty Drive, Suite 200
Bloomington, IN 47403
www.authorhouse.com
Phone: 1-800-839-8640

AuthorHouse™ UK Ltd.
500 Avebury Boulevard
Central Milton Keynes, MK9 2BE
www.authorhouse.co.uk
Phone: 08001974150

This book is a work of non-fiction. Unless otherwise noted, the author
and the publisher make no explicit guarantees as to the accuracy of
the information contained in this book and in some cases, names
of people and places have been altered to protect their privacy.

First published by AuthorHouse 8/15/2006

ISBN: 1-4259-5214-3 (e)
ISBN: 1-4259-5213-5 (sc)

Library of Congress Control Number: 2006906491

Printed in the United States of America
Bloomington, Indiana

This book is printed on acid-free paper.

Contents

Preface

Know Someone?

Do you know someone who makes bad choices but should know better? Do good people make bad choices? Have you ever tried to help someone who was down on their luck; a family member or someone at work? Have you ever known someone with a giving heart who always seemed to come out on the short end? Can you think of someone you know who really needs help, right now? I have never met a person who did not have a relative in the shadows of destruction, in one form or another. Do you have one?

Then you have picked up the keys to their future! Their destiny is right now, in your very hands.

Bold statement? You bet! But I am confident that, by the time you are through reading this book, you will agree.

Eighty-five percent of us grew up in broken homes, and with that comes many dysfunctional habits that linger on through life, creating disaster after disaster. Then, as we grow, we are determined to do better, but our lives seem to stay on a rollercoaster; up one day, down the next; up one week, down the next.

Ever wondered why? Was it the way I was raised? Maybe it is just me. Could it be God? Question after question runs through our minds at every down turn.

Then, to make it worse, you have people depending on you. Money is an amplifier. If you have more, you can do more! Who could you help, if you had more to help with?

Have you ever known someone that could not handle money well? Could it be they never learned to work properly? All work and no play makes Jack a dull boy; but all play and little work makes Jack have his lights turned off, leave his wife and children, and a multitude of other destructive things.

Within the pages of this small book, you will find the keys to unlock their future. I am a firm believer that a person does not get up in the morning and say, "I am going to screw up today." You cannot make me believe that people want to mess up on purpose.

I have heard many say, "But they know better than that." I have even heard it said of women in battered shelters and of addicts in rehabs. But I can say most assuredly that "habits will keep you where good sense can't reach you." Could it be that the destructive or unproductive habit began because of something much deeper?

As I taught and coached in a women's shelter for several years, some of the greatest victories came when a person could honestly answer the question, "Do you have the habit, or does the habit have you?"

Our little class grew and grew. On many nights in the living room of that little shelter, we had more guests than women in the shelter, from lady Sunday school teachers, pastors' wives, and college students working on social or psychology majors. I will never forget the night that a wealthy lady who had returned to college to complete her masters came to our class. By the night's end, our shelter ladies were ministering to her needs.

The one-hour class most often would run well into the late night, and eventually, as our ladies moved on, we grew into the Back Door Church.

It is our purpose, with this little book, to manifest strength, courage, and wisdom in the hearts and minds of those in need, and to equip those who teach, coach, and minister with the "Invisible Keys" that unlock destiny.

Introduction

Satan's Prison Camp

We shook her and shook her! We screamed to the top of our lungs, "YOU WILL NOT DIE! IN THE NAME OF JESUS, YOU WILL NOT DIE!"

The small child coughed and opened her eyes! The mother had fainted as soon as we brought the little girl up from the bottom of the pool. She had been found after a frantic search for the lost child, which had lasted over an hour. She had been dead for some time. The body was already deep blue and stiffening.

When her eyes opened, her color returned, and she burst from the ground like she had been shot. She looked for her mother and ran as fast as she could through the crowd.

The crowd was elated and awestruck, because God had just raised the dead right before their eyes! Some were singing and shouting the glorious praises to a God they knew. Others were just sitting back, weeping for what they had just been a part of.

We thought the child running to her mother was a normal responsive action, but as the mother was revived, the child was still frantically trying to communicate something to her mother. As we got the crowd and the child down to a moderate, calm state, the child revealed to us what she saw on the other side of death that made her so frantic toward her mother.

Her story goes as follows:

"Mommy, mommy, I saw you behind bars! I tried to get to you, but I couldn't! There was this big, black, shadow man, kinda like a ghost, but it was real!

"He was like a guard. He kept walking up and down the long hallway, and said to each person in every jail cell, 'If I go down, you're going with me.'

"When he came to your jail cell and said it to you, I saw you sink down and cry. I tried to get to you, but I couldn't. I kept calling to you, but you couldn't hear me.

"Then this giant man in a white robe came up to me and said, 'Arise, little girl. I will take you to your mother.' As we walked through this super-gigantic garden, he told me about you and the other people that were in what he called 'The Prison Camp of the Free.' He wrote down a lot of stuff on a piece of paper and gave it to me. He told me that it was the key to unlock the doors of every jail cell, and that I had to give it to each person, because only they could use it to unlock their cell; that another person could not unlock it for them."

The mother and listening crowd quickly asked where the paper was.

She then said, "When he gave the paper to me, he laid it on my head, and it melted into my hair, like running under the garden hose. I felt my head get heavy, and he touched me and said, 'It's time to go.'

"I opened my eyes and saw everybody. Then I saw you and came running to get you. Mommy, I don't want you locked up! And those other people, you have to let them get loose, too! There was a man in the cell next to yours. Mommy, he was a big man. He was bigger than the shadow man! He looked so strong that he could have knocked the bars down, but when the shadow man walked by and said that to him, he just turned his back. It was like he wasn't going to listen. But, Mommy, if he stays in the cell, when the shadow man goes down, he will carry him with him!

"Mommy, we have to help!"

We couldn't believe what we were hearing, but we could not afford not to believe. As the mother and child were members of our Back Door Church, we have been wonderfully blessed to watch them grow, and to record the writings of this child with the key.

And in her own words: "Take this key and give it to those that are in the 'Prison Camp of the Free.'

Chapter One

Hell On Earth

ONE NIGHT, as our little girl knelt down at the altar to pray for a couple who had came into the food pantry earlier that week, she started to rock and weave like she was about to faint. The couple just fell out! I mean, kerplunk!

We rush over to grab our little girl, who was now about ten years of age, but seemed to be surrounded by some kind of force field. Three people almost reached her, but they joined the couple on the floor. I decided I would take another approach.

She started to speak over the couple, so I motioned to the sound man to start the recorder. Her words were like lightning and thunder! I never heard an adult speak with such confidence and command, let alone a child of ten.

Her words are as follows:

"You are trapped! You are in the Prison Camp of the Free. You are experiencing Hell on Earth. You have been bound from birth; you have never known freedom, and freedom scares you. With freedom comes many new choices, and you are afraid of failure.

"I see your jailer. I see his helpers, and you have been obedient to every command they said to you. You don't have any control over your life. Your health is failing. You are bound by a curse of poverty. You hold onto bad habits for security. You are trapped.

"You are trapped in the spirit, and your outside world reflects the turmoil of the your inside world. If you have a runny nose, it is an outward sign of an inward condition. If you have a headache, in is an outward sign of an inward condition. If you don't pay your bills, it is an outward sign of an inward condition. If you do pay your bills, it is an outward sign of an inward condition. If you live in lack, it is an outward sign of an inward condition. If you live with bad habits, it is an outward sign of an inward condition. If you live in poor health, it is an outward sign of an inward condition.

"If you are bound and trapped in the Prison Camp of the Free, if you are experiencing Hell on Earth, it is an outward sign of an inward condition.

"You cannot receive the key to your cell until you can see the key to your cell. Are you ready to look inside?"

I really don't know what happened next. It was like the force field exploded! The sound system went out, and so did the rest of us.

When we regained our whereabouts, the couple had vanished. We didn't know if they came to before us, or if the Lord had taken them away. All we could say was that they were nowhere to be found.

Chapter Two

The Key

BY NOW, our little girl had grown into a lovely young lady of fourteen. Our Back Door Church for the people who didn't feel they fit in with the front-door Christian crowd, had grown some what.

We had seen marvelous healings, deliverances, and miracles; most of which came at the laying on of hands by our lovely young lady. God had blessed her with gifts, and at the time, we had no idea what he was going to do through her.

One evening, a young man came forward for prayer for his back. He was a very handsome, strong, country-looking boy. He said that he hurt his back while working on a car. Our young lady came forward to pray for him; and what happened next, I did not like, I still don't like, and I really did not appreciate God acting as if he ran the place. (Even though He does). I don't know of any minister who has been trained for this. It only comes with "on-the-job" training.

As she stretched forth her hands and began to pray, the young man seemed to be caught by an unseen force that dragged him to the ground. Then, like a worm that had been placed in a frying pan, he appeared to be being burnt from below.

I can still remember it like it was yesterday, and I still don't like it. As the young man lay twisting on the floor, I can remember calling two strong men to help me get him to the back room. The thought crossed my mind that he was doing it for attention. As we reached to lift him from the floor, it was like he weighted two thousand pounds. Without any exaggeration, I can say that the three of us could not lift him with all our might. So, there I stood, with God working on this young man and apparently working on me, too. If I haven't told you yet, I didn't like it.

I turned to our young lady and said, "Now what?"

She staggered toward me, and the rest of this story comes from our very smart sound man who had learned by then to keep the recorder going.

Her words are as follows:

"You cannot hide from the truth! Truth is an honest judge. He will always search the thought and intent of the heart. His arm is not short, nor his ear deaf. His eyes are always open, and there is nowhere to hide.

"You have been arrested by our great and mighty judge, Truth. Now confess the truth and be freed, or refuse and be bound forever. You are not in the Prison Camp of the Free! You are snared by the blood of the innocent.

"Hear my words, because you will not receive a second call to repent. Death and life are in the power of your tongue. By your words, you shall be set free, or by your words you shall be bound. The sower soweth the word. God is not mocked; whatsoever a man soweth, that shall he reap.

"If you hold fast to your sin, you shall have the rewards of sin. Do you hear my words?"

The young man must not have responded correctly for her liking.

She struck the man with both hands on the sides of his head and said, "Receive the truth, and the truth will set you free."

I never saw that young man again. And it was too much for some people in the church, also. I was sitting in my office a week later, meditating on the event, when an associate burst through the door and said, "YOU'RE NOT GOING TO BELIEVE IT! YOU'RE SIMPLY NOT GOING TO BELIEVE IT!"

He threw the local paper across my desk and said, "Look at the front page." There he was, the young man from the floor. The front page said: "Man Confesses Horrible Sin."

As the story went, the young man came forward to confess his sin, because he had an encounter with God. The story further said that they would be checking him out for insanity. I don't believe they trusted his confession about God.

He went to jail a free man, because the Truth had set him free. I turned to my associate and said, "Remind me never to play checkers with God. You never know when he is going to jump you."

Chapter Three

Freeing the Spirit

AS TIME went on, our little lady had grown into a lovely young woman. Her compassion for others never seemed to end. She continued to find new ways to help, and as it is in most church settings, some ways of helping those in need always seemed to rub the frozen chosen the wrong way.

Church politics is what most people call religion, and what the rest of the world calls the church. Those of us in the church can clearly divide the church, into the believers, and religion, which are those who love power and attention.

But the rest of the world sees the church as just another political-minded business seeking to express and impose its own will or agenda.

It was bound to happen. Jesus said that religious leaders would always try to stop the anointed ones, because they can't totally control or own them. So trouble was bound for our lovely young lady, just as history is bound to the page.

The meeting was called to discuss the work of the food ministry and the Back Door Church. Most churches did not want a ministry that broke even financially, let alone one that might cost a little for lights and heat, if it didn't add members who tithed. And to be honest, the frozen chosen didn't make the people coming from the Back Door Church feel welcomed in the front of the church at all. They were called all kinds of names, from "road trash," to "why bothers," "street people," "black sheep," "sorry, low lives" and "high-maintenance."

The meeting was called to order. All the big dogs were there, including the state and district presbytery, as well as all of the elect frozen chosen. The food ministry and the Back Door Church were started by the oldest member of the church, an elderly mother of the faith. She and her husband, before he graduated to go home to the Lord, had ministered to the homeless for years, and were always the cornerstone of the church.

As each member addressed the issue, she shot each of them down, one by one. Her response was, "Over the years of this ministry, did you ever give money? Did you ever give help? Did you ever give advice? Then sit down and shut up." That kind of put it where it belonged.

Then one of the young ministers stood up and said, " I move to close the doors on the entire ministry." At that, our lovely young lady burst to her feet and said, "NO, YOU WON'T!"

This stunned the whole place. She continued, "No, you won't, and I will tell you why. God has promised, by an oath, that man will reap what he sows, and you do not want to harvest hell!"

There was a moment of stunned silence. An elder presbytery stood and asked her to come forward. You have to watch the old guys, they're sharp. You never seem to know which side of the fence they are on. He asked her to come forward and share with them what she saw in the Spirit that the rest of them just couldn't seem to see.

Her words are as follows:

"Brothers and sisters, Pay close attention to what you have planned in your heart concerning the ministry conducted at your back door. At the back door of your church, we minister not only to the needs of the people, but to their spirits and souls, which is more precious to our Lord than all the money you own combined. We minister to eighty-percent women at the back door. May I have liberty to address the ladies here today?"

The elder presbytery said yes.

At that, our lovely young lady turned to the audience and began. "Ladies, from zero to five years of age, what do you remember about your life? Was it good or bad?"

After a moment of small talk they all seemed to agree that they only remembered what they had been told, so they would have to say, "Mostly good."

"Then, let us look at how you developed into the person you have become. From five years of age until fifteen years old, how would you describe your life? Good, bad, or extremely challenging?

You could tell by the dropping of heads and the long silence that everyone was deep in thought. It seemed to apply to the men, as well as to the ladies.

Our lovely young lady continued, "Many of you, as well as those who come to the back door, developed your character and personality by forced exposure to difficult, if not abusive, circumstances and people. You were forced to play a role in the play called history, on a stage called Earth, and you developed your character and personality by the pressures and demands of those around you; forced to play a part that was demonic, wicked, and the victim.

"If I am speaking truth then say Amen."

"AMEN! AMEN!" The whole crowd responded.

She continued, "Then, from fifteen years old until twenty-five years of age, which is the 'choices' stage of your life, you ride a rollercoaster. Life is up one week, then down the next; up one month, and down the next. And most people crash land on planet Earth during that period, because from five to fifteen is the teaching stage, whereby we load our minds with information. Having less than adequate information and playing the character role that was forced upon us, our outside world reflects back to us the rewards due to the character we play, and crashing and burning is the normal screenplay at the third stage of your life.

"We have a women here today who were forced to play a horrible role during the ages of five to fifteen. At the hands of wicked men and even a wicked father, the role she was forced to play was that of sexual abuse. Then, as she grew away from home, the wardrobe and character went with her.

It was not a character of her choice or a character that our heavenly Father designed; but here we have her playing the only part in the play called history that she knows how to play.

"How is she redeemed? How is she to be saved from a sure hell? How is her spirit to be set free from the bondages of these years of pressure and torment?"

By now, some of the women in the crowd were crying.

"Let me go deeper, if I may. Twenty-five to forty years of age is the recovery stage. You have finally figured out that the rewards of certain behaviors are less than desirable. You have spent years playing the part of a secret whore and concubine of wicked men who are playing a role that they, too, were taught to play. You firmly make up your mind that you are not going to continue to be treated that way. But over and over again, you can't seem to find the way out of bondage.

"If you will allow me just a few more moments, I will express our concerns for the next stage of life, and then I will summarize what I see in the Spirit."

The elder presbytery said, "Sister, please feel free."

"The curtains are opened to the fifth stage of life. From ages forty to sixty-five, the performance is titled, 'Significant.' This is the stage of life that becomes, 'Make it or break it.' A man during these years, as many of you are here today, must feel that you are making an impact, and that you are significant. And if you do not feel important at work, then you must receive it at church. If not at church, then at some hobby. But if not through some other means, then your wife must make you feel important, or we will hear a story like I heard just a few days ago at the back door of your church.

"A well-accomplish businesswomen had heard of our minister and had no one she could talk to. She did not come for food, nor any of the other common ministries; simply to find the strength of God's eternal wisdom. Her husband had been gone for several days, and she didn't know why he left. As I described the stage of life that she and he were going through, and that if he did not feel important at home, then he would find some very immature people, probably a woman, to surround himself with.

"She began to cry and said, then, 'I know where to find him.' I continued to minister the strategy of God's wisdom and the proper course of conduct was agreed upon. Then I ministered to her spirit; the role or character she was playing.

"I ask you here today the same thing that I asked her. If you can change the role in life you are playing that is expressed through your personality and actions, would you?"

Many in the audience, and two ministers on the platform, spontaneously said yes.

"Then the light of the Gospel, the great Holy Spirit of God, the burden-remover and yoke-destroyer, stands here right now to confirm His Word with signs and wonders. At the cross, all men were set free. A slave or a prisoner does not have a choice, but when we shine the Light of God into your spirit, and you can, for the first time in your life, see that you have a choice, you become free. Free to choose.

"Whom the Son sets free is free indeed.

"The Light of God's Word has shown you that you can no longer be controlled by something you now have control over. Jesus said, 'Now that I have come, they have no more cloak for their sin'

"In summary, my dear brothers and sisters, these people are like most of you. They are in the Prison Camp of the Free, but they do not have the key to their cell. It is not only our duty before God to set the captive free, it is also our message to the world that Jesus is the High Priest, the Author and Finisher of our Faith; that He is the resurrection and the life, and that any who come to him will not be ashamed, nor turned away.

"Gentlemen, what would you say if a hospital closed its doors to those in need, or a police officer who saw a tragic accident went on his way without rendering assistance? What would God say to a man who saw a women or man set on fire with the flames of hell and refused to throw the bucket of water that he held in his hand? Would he not surely harvest the full wrath of God? The full measure of the torments of Hell?

"Brothers and sisters, you may look at a ministry through the eyes of cost. You may look at it through the eyes of number of members it generates. You may even look at it through the eyes of work, worry, and headaches. But I ask you to look at it through the eyes of a loving father, and through the eyes of our Eternal Judge, who will judge the quick and the dead by the thoughts and intents of our hearts."

She turned and walked back to her seat.

The elder presbytery stood, with bible in hand, and walked to the podium. He began, "Today, I have heard the Word and Voice of God concerning this matter. Brothers, you may bring this matter to a vote if you wish. But as for me and my house, the word of God is not a voting matter."

At that, he walked down from the platform, was joined by his wife in the aisle, and left the church without another word.

The other ministers followed suit. The meeting was never officially closed, and it did not appear in the official record as ever taking place. The only ones who remained in the crowd were a few men and women, with their hearts on fire from years of torment; and our lovely young lady and elderly mother of faith were more than happy to supply the living water to quench the blaze.

Chapter Four

Freeing the Soul

A FEW WEEKS later, the phone rang at the food ministry. Our elder mother of faith answered and said, "Yes, sir. She is right here, but I am sure the answer will be yes."

She called to our lovely young lady and asked, "Would you minister to a women's conference next week?"

"For who and where?" she asked.

"For our favorite presbytery and his wife. It is only about a two-hour drive."

"Tell them I would love to do anything I could to help."

A couple of days before our lovely young lady was to minister, she walked into my office with a look of concern. I asked what was on her mind. She was concerned that the upcoming meeting would be the first time she ever ministered outside our church. She wanted me to help her to frame a message.

I studied her face for a moment. I knew that her calling was not that of a preacher, so I waited for God to quicken me on how to address her concern.

As the thought came to mind, I began, "Your calling is not that of a preacher or specifically that of a teacher, so it would be unlikely that you will ever be give a framed or outlined message in the normal sense. Let me explain; the prophet is given a vivid vision of what God says is to happen, and then shares the vision as articulately as is possible for that time and culture. Those of us who can see what he or she is saying have caught the vision. The evangelist then enters the field of that vision and plows long and hard in the hardened hearts of the soil of the souls that God seeks. Then the apostles organize the bodies and set in place the churches. Preachers are set in place by God to care for the body of believers, and to sow the Word. Then teachers are raised up to water the Word that has been sown in the garden of God.

"You have read the scripture; 'many are called, but few are chosen?'"

"Yes, sir."

"You, my child are chosen. You are chosen of God to harvest souls. You are to walk into the field of God that another has plowed, another has sown, and another has well-watered; and harvest the souls for God.

"Even if you and I were to write the world's greatest sermon or teaching, you would never be able to deliver it, even if you studied for its delivery a month, because your calling is for souls, and as soon as you start to deliver a message, you will discern and see their souls, and you would jump off the train of thought and run into the field. The specific train of thought is not the priority of the event, nor should it ever be. The priority is to deliver to our God the souls that he paid such a high price for."

At that, she returned to the food ministry to help the others.

As they drove into the parking lot of the church, they were surprised to see three buses with the names of other churches on the side, and several police cars around a prison bus. They were an hour early, and already having a tough time finding a parking place.

They walked into the lobby and were instantly spotted by the pastor's wife. She ran up, hugged them, and said, "We have never seen such a crowd. My husband just told a few pastors who were at that council meeting, and look at what the Lord is doing!"

Our lovely young lady started feeling a little uneasy in her stomach. Our elderly mother noticed and whispered in her ear, "God has sent you here for one person. Find that person, minister to them, and we are out of here."

That seemed to occupy our lovely young lady's mind. She had never known the battles of thought that went on in the mind of a minister just before they entered the field.

The pastor's wife said that the other wives and pastors were in the office, and she led them through the halls. As they entered the room, everyone started speaking at the same time. They laughed and hugged, then began explaining how the meeting became so large.

The elder presbytery began: "You may recognize our pastors from the meeting at your church. The reason that I and my wife left so abruptly from the meeting that day was because, while you were speaking, our eyes and minds met, and we instantly knew that we had a church full of people in the Prison Camp of the Free, and God had just revealed, through you, the key to set them free; and she and I were not going to waste one minute in doing so."

Unable to contain himself, another pastor jumped in, "We, too, dove directly into the work. We have seen miracle-life transformation!

Another wife began, "Our church has became like a mobile army. Every person, from the oldest to the least, who has receive this revelation, has been given the Holy Ghost's power to minister to family and friends. They feel the power of God working through them when the people they are ministering to change into a new creature right before their eyes."

The elder pastor moved in. "That's right. Within days of a person being brought into the light of the gospel and seeing that they can shape and mold the role or character they play, they develop an awesome sense of power and control. They see that God is a creator, and His children are to be creators of destiny as well."

The elder's wife began, "We have run into some roadblocks, and as we sought God on them, we all felt that He was leading us to you."

Sensing that everyone in the room was many years her elder, our lovely young lady said, "I must be honest with everyone here, this is my first time to minister outside my church, and it seems somewhat overwhelming."

The elder pastor started again. "I spoke to your pastor earlier today, and he told me what he spoke to you about, and we all agree with his assessment. You are called to harvest souls. Let me share with you an old pastor's trick to calm the nerves: just think that God has called you here to minister to just one person, and occupy your mind with looking for that one person, and you'll do just fine."

Our lovely young lady gave our elder mother of faith a look that everyone in the room caught onto, and they began to laugh.

"So," said the pastor's wife, "She had already tried to calm your nerves?"

The pastor looked at his watch and said, "It's time to get started." At that, everyone left the room, and the pastor walked the young lady up onto the stage.

The introduction of our lovely young lady was met with a standing ovation, which added to her uneasiness; but as soon as she stepped behind the podium, all fear was gone.

The message here is condensed but her words are as follows:

You Can't Build Your Future on the Foundation of Your Past

I am overwhelmed with joy as I hear what God has done and is doing in your life. There are no words great enough to describe to you the joy bound within my heart in knowing that, in some small way, our great and loving Father has allowed me to work in His field. And as I stand here tonight, I am ever mindful that we all stand before a great and loving Father and an unwavering Judge of Truth.

1 Thessalonians 5:23 gives us the three-fold nature of man: spirit, soul, and body. You are well aware of how to free the spirit. To bring a person's spirit and character into the light of the Gospel, whereby they become free to choose. They are no longer bound by the unseen nature of the spirit that kept them chained to the habits of unhappy or destructive choices. But to-night, we must move closer to freedom by giving you the key to your souls. Just as we brought the spirit, or character, into the light of the gospel, and you were made free to choose life or death, we must also bring the soul into the light of the gospel, so that your choices will be equally clear.

The soul of man is his mind. The mind is the garden, and thoughts are seeds. There has never been an evil man who did not first sow evil seeds in his garden, whereby a plant came forth. The plant is an act or action. When the plant comes forth, then soon to follow is the fruit. The fruit is the reward for the action. The circumstance, whether good or bad, is the fruit of conduct. One must clearly make the connection between the parable of the garden as it mirrors the mind of man, for the light of this truth will bring forth the redeeming virtues of Christ.

An evil man has willfully enjoyed the sowing of evil thoughts into the garden of his mind, and his life becomes completely surrounded by circumstances that, most unknown to him, are the fully ripened fruits that have fallen from the plants that he, himself, has willfully sown in his garden.

On the other hand, we have a man who also is not conscientiously aware of the garden of his mind, but chooses to think on good things. The onlookers think of this man as blessed. They may say he came from a good upbringing. They may call him lucky. But the truth is that he has sown seeds of thought that brought forth good plants of actions, which brought forth fully ripened fruit of circumstances that we may call and see as blessings.

With this truth in full light, let us see the relationship between the spirit, or character, and the soul, or mind. One may say that when my spirit was set free and He gave me a new spirit, that my thinking changed. I would say that you are correct as to your thoughts of your self image. But in the above illumination of both the good man and the evil man, we have not addressed sin. May I submit to you that both men are still subject to spend eternity under the wrath of God.

Most here will most assuredly argue that the good man who thought on good things and yielded good fruit would enter heaven. But that is far, far, from the truth of the gospel. The gospel makes no such claim or promise, neither does it remotely imply such a doctrine of works. The gospel says that a man must die to self. Here in America, the intellectual arena is filled with self-made, self-willing, and high-achievement-minded souls who will spend eternity cursing God for counting them for enemies.

The scriptures say that God is a good God and a loving Father, and that he sends rain on the just and unjust. That means that He sends His Word and Light to all men, so we may be able to set your spirit free and may be able to teach your soul to think on good thoughts, and the soul will still be full of sin.

May the following words that I received from the mouth of God burn in the mind of man for all eternity.

"Father, what is sin?" **S**elf-**I**ntending **N**ature. = S.I.N.

The self-intending nature was born of Satan while in Heaven. The scriptures say that he beheld himself, and that he said he would exalt himself. God cast him down to earth. In the garden, he infected man with this same sickness. Let me illuminate this truth: Adam and Eve were created in the image of God. The image of God is brighter than the noonday sun. When they took of the fruit of self will, the light that illuminated from their bodies went out, and they saw themselves. Self consciousness was brought upon man by Satan. He sowed a thought of self will into the mind of man, and it grew into an act that yielded the fruit of original sin, that we, ourselves, are still under today.

So Jesus will separate the sheep from the goats based on those who have died to self. The prodigal son died to self, but the brother did not. The rich, young ruler thought good thoughts, did good acts, and was abundantly blessed with good fruit, but could not die to self.

To free the soul, one must love someone other than themselves. To free the soul, one must die to self. Your mind is the garden of thought, and you can achieve the highest and best life has to offer, and you should. But hear the words of the Lord: "What will it profit a man if he gains the whole world and looses his soul?"

I rejoice that your spirit is free. And I rejoice that you now see the garden of your mind that can free your soul. But I beg you, die to self, love somebody other than yourself, or you will never escape the Prison Camp of the Free.

Chapter Five

What Hell Can't Hold

THE FOLLOWING MORNING, our lovely young lady and elderly mother of faith had breakfast with the pastors and their wives. They had asked for her to speak at the woman's prison before she left for home.

On the way to the meeting, everyone could sense that something big was going to happen. The meeting hall was standing-room only, and guards lined the walls and halls. The air was warm and humid, because the crowd was much to large for the room, and the air-conditioning unit just could not keep up.

It did not seem to bother our lovely young lady as she was introduced and stepped to the podium. The elder pastor reports the meeting as follows:

"The lovely young lady opened in prayer. The prayer was directed to the throne in a manner uncommon to normal pulpit practices.

"Her words are as follows:

"'Our most loving and giving Father, I come to you today, standing in front of these people, and ask you to speak to me in a way that they cannot deny you have spoken. Many think that you are not a real person. Many think that you were just a person of history. Many here today do not believe you hear and answer prayers.'

"At that, she began walking around and around the podium. On the seventh time around, she came to a sudden stop in front of the podium and pointed toward the audience. All at once, everyone in the room began to weep and cry.

"She became frozen like a statue and began to speak.

"'I am standing in a sandy dessert. In front of me is a large group of men in desert clothing; robes and turbans. We are all standing at the foot of a very high, sandy mountain. They are talking among themselves about the man on top of the mountain. They say he is the greatest archer who has ever lived.

"'"Sirs, Why don't we ask him to teach us to shoot?"

"'They all are moving away from me. They are all afraid of the man on the mountain. I will ask him.

"'The mountain is steep. I am climbing it on my hands and knees. The sand squeezes between my fingers, and my legs are tired. But here I am at the top. There is a man sitting on a stick that is in the shape of a "T." On his back is a quiver with five arrows. Each arrow has different-colored feathers. He has a longbow that looks like that of a tribe.

"'"Sir, Will you teach me to shoot?"

"'He has turned toward me. His skin is very weather-worn. There are a lot of battle scars on his face and arms. He has handed me the bow. Now he has handed me an arrow with blue feathers. He has told me to shoot.'

"She looks both right and left. Still in a statue form, she turns all the way around, even though her feet and legs do not move.

"She says, 'At what?' She becomes un frozen and jumps back a few feet, as if something startled her. She continues, 'The vision is gone. I see him no more. The last thing he did was to snatch the bow out of my hand and say, "Come back when you are ready."'"

"She lifts her head toward the ceiling and says, 'Father, I have receive the vision. Please, send the interpretation.' She remained motionless for a moment, then began.

"'If you aim at nothing, you will hit it. Faith is the substance of things hoped for. A life without purpose is a life without any need of faith. Without any demand placed on the 7487 promises He has made to man.

"'Most of you came straight out of school and were under the curse of Cain; a reckless wanderer without a vision, without a goal, without a target. You do not need any help if you are aiming at nothing. A man cannot die who has purpose. The spirit will refuse to leave the body if he has not fulfilled his purpose. Jesus did not fulfill His purpose at the cross, because He had not conquered death, hell, and the grave. So He walked in and picked up His body and walked out to complete what He had purposed in His life.

"'Without faith, it is impossible to please God, because those who come to God must believe that He is and that He is a rewarder of them that diligently seek Him.

"'We may lead you into the Light of God to free your spirit, and we may lead you into the Light of God to free your soul, but it is a complete waste of time to cast our Lord's pearls under the feet of swine. A swine is a reckless wanderer; a person without purpose, without targets, or goals. A person without a destination is a person with no destiny. Tomorrow's air is wasted on your every breath. God's earth is burdened with your foot. Anything that is not of faith is sin.

"'There was a young boy sold into a work camp for a loaf of bread to keep his starving family from death, and he was forced to work in the sewing plant, eighteen hours a day, and he had to sleep by his machine. But in his heart, he had the purpose of helping his family. As the years went on, his purpose grew. He purposed to help free his village from poverty. The purpose grew into a vision, and he meditated therein, day and night, until the four walls of the factory could no longer hold him. He ended up buying that plant and many others. He led his village and many, many others out of wicked poverty and slavery.

"'A man without a purpose will never receive a vision from God. If you aim at nothing, you will hit it. A man without a purpose is already in prison, whether he lives in the suite, or the street.

"'But for a man with a purpose that is not a sin-filled purpose, the walls of any prison are not tall enough to hold him. They are not thick enough to hold him, nor are they strong enough to hold him. For a man with a purpose that is not filled with the Self-Intending Nature, Hell can't hold him.

"'He whom the Son sets free is free indeed. Talk to the archer, and let the arrow of vision fly.

"'Combine the three invisible keys, and you will come out of the Prison Camp of the Free.

"'Free the spirit, free the soul, and free the body. When purpose comes in, the body is free.'"

Chapter Six

He Will Take You With Him

SEVERAL WEEKS PASSED before our lovely young lady seemed like she was back to normal. The meetings appeared to drain her, and we all gave her space to come to grips and to process what had happened to her.

I came in early on the day of the food ministry to find our lovely young lady crying. She just kept saying, "They don't know what is waiting on them."

As our elderly mother of faith arrived, she seemed to understand the words. I felt that I was the only one outside of this deep secret. The elderly mother told me that they had been praying for weeks about how to break through a stronghold that had the minds of most people blinded.

I asked them to explain to me what stronghold and how they could detect it. The lovely young lady began.

"Pastor, eight out of ten people we minister to claim they know Jesus, and that their home is in Heaven, but according to his Word, they have been deceived, and when the shadow man goes down, they will go with him."

It had been many years since I had heard the term, "shadow man," but I knew exactly what she was saying.

She continued, "Even though they live in wickedness that they admit to, and we give them ten specific scriptures to show them the danger they are in, we still can't break through. It is not ignorance. Ignorance is the selective will to ignore, like the big man in the cell next to the one Mom was in, the one who kept turning his back. Pastor, they say they believe in Jesus, but they live their lives as if there was no eternal life and no real judgment. John 3:18 says they are condemned already, because they don't believe."

"Well, child, how will they know they don't want to go if you haven't revealed to them what it is going to be like?"

"Pastor, I'm glad you said that, because that was exactly what I had planned for today, but I did not want you to think I was being mean."

"Just tell them the truth, child. Just tell them the truth."

As the crowd began to come in, I could tell that we were about to enter a new season of ministry. I just could not yet tell what kind of impact that it would have.

By the end of the day, we had people walk out without food, walk out crying, walk out cussing, and a few walked out with smiles. I asked our lovely young lady to walk me through what she had been telling them.

Her words are as follows:

"First, I ask them to describe Heaven to me. Then I asked them to describe Hell. After I listened to them, I would ask if they would like to know how the Bible described Hell. They all said, 'Yeah,' like some kind of joke. Then I would begin by telling them that I would only share three things about Hell, and no matter how many questions they asked, I would not go any further than that. And they said okay.

The first thing was what the Bible says Hell is like. The Bible says the fire is so hot it melts the earth. That means it is so hot it melts rocks. It is also complete and total darkness. Jesus said they will be tied, hand and foot, and cast into total darkness. In Egypt, is was a darkness that could be felt, and it made every thing stand still, and even a candle could not penetrate the darkness; a darkness so dark that light cannot open it. The Bible also teaches that Hell is total fear. You hear cries and moaning forever, and you have nowhere you can go that you can escape the darkness, and nowhere you can go to escape the fear.

"The second thing was what the Bible says about the torments that will be in Hell. The Bible says that the serpent will be biting you. It says that you will gnaw your tongue because of the pain, until it spews out blood, then you will gnaw it more, for the pain never ends. It says that Satan and the demons will jump on you, tear you, and torment you. And if that were not more than you could bear, the Bible says that the wrath and fury of the Almighty God will be upon you without measure and without pity. It says that God will be so mad that He will crush you under his foot until your blood spews on to His clothes, and even then, He will not have any regard for you at all. If that wasn't a million times more than one could bear, there is still an even worse torment; that is to know the love and splendor that was available, and yet in the horrible darkness and fear, engulfed in this furnace of heat, being bitten and torn from things you can't see, being pressed until your body squirts blood in every direction,

49

gnawing and screaming, you will know every sin that brought you to that place.

"The third thing was who the Bible says is going to be in Hell. Jesus said that not everyone who called Him Lord would enter heaven. That means some people who believe they are Christians will go to this place of wrath. He said that those who refuse to believe and be baptized are condemned already. He said those who love the world more than the church will be spewed out of His mouth. He said the wicked servant who had a talent but refused to use it for the kingdom will be cast there. He said that those who refuse to forgive will be turned over to the tormenter, as will anyone who leads the children the wrong way. He said the drunkard, the liar, and the homosexual will be added to the enemies of God. He said that those who engaged in sex outside of marriage will enter into the eternity of darkness, fear, biting, pain, and torment, and forever , through all eternity, be under, every moment of every hour of every day, the fierceness, anger, and wrath of an Almighty God filled with anger, and without pity or mercy.

"Pastor, I really did not tell them much about Hell. I did not think they could bear it. The Bible gets way more graphic than I cared to describe. I just gave them the highlights. At first they thought is was something to laugh at, but after I gave them a brief summary, they did seem a little unsettled. I forgot to tell them that it was not murder or child molestation that got Adam and Eve cast out and separated from God, but just not believing God meant what He said, when He said it."

There wasn't anything left to say but, "You told them the truth." At that, we closed up for the day.

Chapter Seven

The Doorway

THE PHONE rang and woke us from a deep sleep. A minister always gets a deep sinking feeling when the phone rings very late at night. There was a woman's voice on the other end.

"ARE YOU THE PASTOR OF THE BACK DOOR CHURCH? QUICK! ARE YOU THE PASTOR?"

"Yes, I am. Can I help you?"

"YOU HAVE TO GET THAT LADY WHO SPOKE TO MY BOYFRIEND TODAY OVER HERE, RIGHT AWAY!"

"Calm down, and tell me what is going on. It is 2 a.m. in the morning. I can't call and get her up. How can I help?"

"YOU DON'T UNDERSTAND! HE'S DYING! HE SAID HE HAS TO SPEAK TO HER, AND HE HAS TO SPEAK TO HER RIGHT NOW, BEFORE IT'S TOO LATE.. PLEASE, PASTOR, YOU HAVE TO GET HER OVER HERE!"

"First, who are you? Secondly, where are you? And who else is with you, and why is he dying?"

"I AM the girl whose boyfriend left the food pantry today, cussing everybody out, and we live a half mile from the church, but we are at the hospital. I am here with my boyfriend, and they say he is not going to make it another hour. He was in a bad car wreck. All he wants is to talk to that lady. Please, please. Will you help me?

"Okay, I'll phone her, and we will be right there!"

Our young lady said that the Lord had gotten her up about an hour earlier, and she knew she was to pray for someone, but didn't know who. We drove into the parking lot, parked, and rushed right in.

The woman on the phone met us at the door.

"HE'S LEAVING US! HE WANTS TO SPEAK TO YOU BEFORE HE GOES."

We walked into the room, and a nurse looked up at us and shook her head. She said to the young man, "I told you she would be here. Here she is." The nurse turned to our lovely young lady, addressed her by name, and said, "He's been holding on, because I promised him that you would be here. The ER desk misplaced your number, or we wouldn't have had to call the pastor."

I felt a little out of place. Apparently, our lovely young lady came there quite often to have her phone number on file.

She stepped up to the young man and began: "Hi, my friend, I'm here, and Jesus is with me. What can we do?"

He had bandages everywhere, and he could only look with one eye, and it looked as if it was about to drop out. He said, "I went through the windshield. I would have been fine, but the devil put a tree in my way."

She responded, "He has been known to do that."

He coughed and rolled his head to the side so he could see her face to face; and as long as I live, I will never forget what he said: "I'm about to go to Hell, ain't I?"

I had never seen her in this depth of ministry before, and yet she seemed as if she had handled this every day. She said, "Not if Jesus and I have anything to do about it, you won't."

A tear rolled down from his one eye as he said, "Every word you said today about Hell was true, and everything but molesting a child and homosexuality, I have done. I am going to Hell, and I know I deserve it."

She gripped his hand a little tighter and said, "Before you go, can I ask you a few questions?"

"You can ask me anything, and I will tell you the truth," he said.

She continued, "If you could go to heaven, would you?"

He stared at her for a small moment, as if to see if she was trying to con him. Street people are hard to con; they can read the lines on your face, so you have to shoot straight with them. He said, "I don't see it happening, but yes, I would."

She said, "I went to a funeral of a six-year-old girl who went through a windshield because her dad went to sleep while driving. Do you think she was innocent?"

"I can't see where she did anything wrong," he said.

"Then you can see innocent blood. Even though you have not lived right, you can still recognize innocent blood. Well then, there is still hope for you," she said.

He again coughed and said, "I don't understand."

She continued, "Mary had a little lamb whose fleece was white as snow. One day when Mary came home, Moses said the lamb had to go. You see, in the Old Testament, Moses told the children of Israel that death was going to come by their houses that night, and the only way to keep him from coming in was to have innocent blood over the top and down the sides of their door. So, since they had all done wrong in their lives, they had to use the innocent blood of a lamb. When death came by, He would not cross the innocent blood line."

"What does that have to do with me?" he asked.

"Do you think Jesus did anything wrong or sinned in any way?" she asked.

He said, "If He did, I can't see it."

"There you go again. You can recognize innocent blood. Do you think if the children of Israel would have put the blood of Jesus over their doors, that Death would have crossed the innocent blood line?" she pressed the question.

He seem to be engulfed in the scene, "The devil himself wouldn't do that!"

She pressed on, "You see it, pretty much, just like I do. And in the Old Testament, their door was the door to a house, but in the New Testament, Jesus says that your door is the door of your heart. And if you want to be joined to Jesus, you have to put innocent blood over your door before death comes by."

He hung on every word. "How do I do that?" he asked.

"Just walk through the door," she said, "Just walk through the door. Jesus said, 'I am the doorway. No man comes to the Father except by me. And if any man comes to me, I will in no way cast him out.' If you believe Jesus is the Son of God, He was sinless, and he gave his blood for you to put over the door of your heart, then the doorway is open to you. Just walk through the door. Heaven is yours."

He was crying, but he managed to ask, "Why did he do that for me"?

She smiled and said, "You'll have to come to Bible class on Thursday nights to find that out."

He coughed again and said, "Don't think I'll make it."

She stood up and asked, "And just why not? Too good to be seen around the back door of a church?"

"Aren't you forgetting?" he asked.

"I thought you put the innocent blood over the door of your heart," she puzzled.

He responded, "I did!"

"Then death can't enter. What are you going to do when you get out of the hospital?" she questioned.

He turned to his girlfriend, "If I live, will you marry me and we'll learn about who Jesus is?"

She burst into tears and ran to him saying, "Yes, yes, yes!"

As we turned to leave the room, our lovely young lady said, "See you both at class." And we walked out to the nurse's desk.

The ER doctor came around the corner. He saw our lovely young lady at the desk. "Is he going to make it?" he asked.

"Oh, Yeah!" said our lovely young lady. "Death left the room about five minute ago. He will be fine."

The doctor never broke stride. As he started down the hall, he called to the head nurse, "Call upstairs and get his room ready."

I thought to myself, You know, a pastor should probably get out more at night. No telling what his congregation is doing.

The head nurse rounded the desk and gave our lovely young lady a great big hug. The nurse looked at me and said, "If it wasn't for this young lady, I would still have MS."

Well, I just couldn't hold back anymore. "What in the world have you been doing all these years, behind my back?"

Three nurses and two interns began to laugh. The head nurse asked, "You didn't know she moonlights as a saint?"

I chuckled, but she continued, "I had MS so badly that if I sat down in a chair, someone had to get me out. She prayed for me one night when

I was up here for treatment, and I sat down on the floor and got up several times. I was healed of MS right there, on that floor, and everyone here saw it. The doc who just passed told me that, as soon as I gained my weight back, that I could come to work. That was four years ago."

All I could do was smile. But she wasn't going to let me off so easily. "The first week I was back at work, she was here one night when they brought in a little girl, about four years old, wearing a body cast, and whose parents the doctors had told that she would never walk. This place came unglued that night when the little girl ran back and forth across the lobby. Then there was the real heavy-set lady who had been in a wheelchair for nine years. She left pushing the thing."

"Young lady," I said, "why haven't you told us anything about these miracles?"

She responded, "I thought you were doing them somewhere else. You always preached on them."

There wasn't much I could say, and the other nurses were reminding the head nurse of another miracle.

The head nurse opened a drawer and pulled out a picture. "See this little baby? Her mother was in here for a procedure to remove the baby, because it was dead in her womb. Your lovely young lady and an elderly lady from your church laid hands on her stomach and prayed, and God restored life to the child. And if that isn't enough, when the child was born, it was under two pounds. When she came out, all five doctors agreed it was a miracle, because the umbilical cord had detached, and the baby had lived inside the mother without any life support. Without the cord, it is impossible. But that baby is over two years old now."

After I dropped off our lovely young lady at four thirty in the morning, I went walking down to the church. As I sat near the back door and watched the sun open another page in the lives of man, I saw the big shadow of a tree in the distance, swaying back and forth in front of a picket fence that looked like the bars on a jail cell, and my mind raced back to the story of a little girl who saw a jailer she called "the shadow man."

About the Authors

Dean and Tammie Carter are known worldwide for their stand against American Terrorism and Racism in the 1987 Brotherhood Marches commemorating Dr. Martin Luther King's first federal holiday. Having addressed issues of race, culture, and social change, Dean and Tammie have had an impact on people's lives around the world and have been fondly named, "Freedom Fighters".

Dean received the honored, "Drum Major for Justice" award from the Southern Christian Leadership Conference, and some of his most cherished memories are speaking from Mr. King's pulpit at Ebenezer Baptist Church, and marching arm in arm with history, Mrs. Coretta Scott King.

Tammie's ministry to women in jails, rehabs, pantries, and shelters, has altered the course of countless lives. Being thrown into a trash pile and left to die by her addict mother, at two days of age, Tammie was rescued by God to set women free from generational curses and the spirit of rejection.

Dean, at age twelve made his home under bridges, brings a sense of faith, focus, follow through, and forgiveness to a nation of men under the curse of the fatherless.

Being featured in documentaries and books for effectively creating environments of change, Dean and Tammie's impact on people and communities will be felt for decades to come.

Outreach Christian Ministry, lead by Dean and Tammie Carter is an evangelical outreach. From feeding the hungry to helping churches build high impact teams, Dean, Tammie, and their three sons are impacting lives with the **"IN-VISIBLE KEYS"**

For information on
Dean and Tammie Carter
and Outreach Christian Ministry
contact

Tammie@outreachchristianministry.org
678 283 4796